BELIEVE *Acoustic*

ISBN 978-1-4803-4222-4

HAL•LEONARD®
CORPORATION

7777 W. BLUEMOUND RD. P.O. BOX 13819 MILWAUKEE, WI 53213

Visit Hal Leonard Online at
www.halleonard.com

BOYFRIEND

Words and Music by JUSTIN BIEBER,
MAT MUSTO, MIKE POSNER
and MASON LEVY

Lyrics:
If I was your boy-friend, I'd nev-er let you go, I can take you plac-es you ain't ev-er been be-fore.

Ba-by, take a chance or you'll nev-er ev-er know, I got mon-ey in my hands that I'd real-ly like to blow,

As Long As You Love Me

Words and Music by JUSTIN BIEBER,
SEAN ANDERSON, NASRI ATWEH,
RODNEY JERKINS and ANDRE LINDAL

13

As long as you love ___ me, you love ___ me, you love ___

___ me, yeah. ___ As long as you love ___ me, ___ yeah.

Additional Lyrics

Vocal ad lib: I don't know if this makes sense but you're my hallelujah.
Give me a time and place, I'll rendezvous it. I'll fly you to ya.
I'll beat you there. Girl, you know I got you.
Us, trust, a couple things I can't spell without you. Now we on top of the world.
That's just how we do. Used to tell me, "sky's the limit", now the
sky's our point of view. Now, we steppin' out like, "Oh God."
Camera's point and shoot. Ask me what's my best side. I stand back and point at you.
You, you the one that I argue with. Feel like I need a new girl to be bothered with.
But the grass ain't always greener on the other side, it's green where you water it.
So I know we got issues baby, true, true, true but I'd rather work on this with you
than to go ahead and start with someone new.

BEAUTY AND A BEAT

Words and Music by JUSTIN BIEBER,
NICKI MINAJ, MAX MARTIN,
ANTON ZASLAVSKI and SAVAN KOTECHA

SHE DON'T LIKE THE LIGHTS

Words and Music by JUSTIN BIEBER,
TIYON "TC" MACK, RODNEY JERKINS
and ANDRE LINDAL

Recorded a half-step lower

TAKE YOU

Words and Music by JUSTIN BIEBER,
RAPHAEL JURDIN, PIERRE-ANTOINE MELKI,
ROSS GOLAN, JAMES ABRAHART,
ALEXANDER DEZEN and B. MADDAHI

Acoustic Pop

Hey, what's the sit-u-a-tion? Oh._____ I'm just
ta-tion. Oh._____ It's

try'n' to make a lit-tle con-ver-sa-tion. Why the hes-i-ta-tion? Oh._____
on-ly me and you in this e-qua-tion. Prom-ise this oc-ca-sion. Oh._____

——— Tell me what your name is. For your in-for-ma-tion, don't get___ me
——— It's a dif-f'rent sit-u-a-tion. For your in-for-ma-tion, don't get___ me

BE ALRIGHT

Words and Music by JUSTIN BIEBER
and DAN KANTER

ALL AROUND THE WORLD

Words and Music by JUSTIN BIEBER,
NASRI ATWEH, CHRISTOPHER BRIDGES,
ADAM MESSINGER and NOLAN LAMBROZZA

FALL

Words and Music by JUSTIN BIEBER,
MASON LEVY and JASON LUTRELL

YELLOW RAINCOAT

Words and Music by
JUSTIN BIEBER

With movement

'Cause I put on my rain - coat, my yel - low rain - coat.

Ba - by, it's keep - ing me dry. _____ I put on my rain - coat,

my yel - low rain - coat, you know ex - act - ly why. _____ When the

my yel-low rain-coat. Ba-by, it's keep-ing me dry._____ I

put on my rain-coat, my yel-low rain-coat, you know ex-act-ly why.

Repeat and Fade

Optional Ending

I WOULD

Words and Music by JUSTIN BIEBER,
AARON MICHAEL COX, SEAN FENTON,
MARCOS PALACIOS, ERNEST CLARK
and MARCUS MOODY

With a moderate groove

NOTHING LIKE US

Words and Music by
JUSTIN BIEBER

There's noth - ing like us, there's noth - ing like

you and me _____ to - geth - er.

slowly